The MACK'N ALMANAC

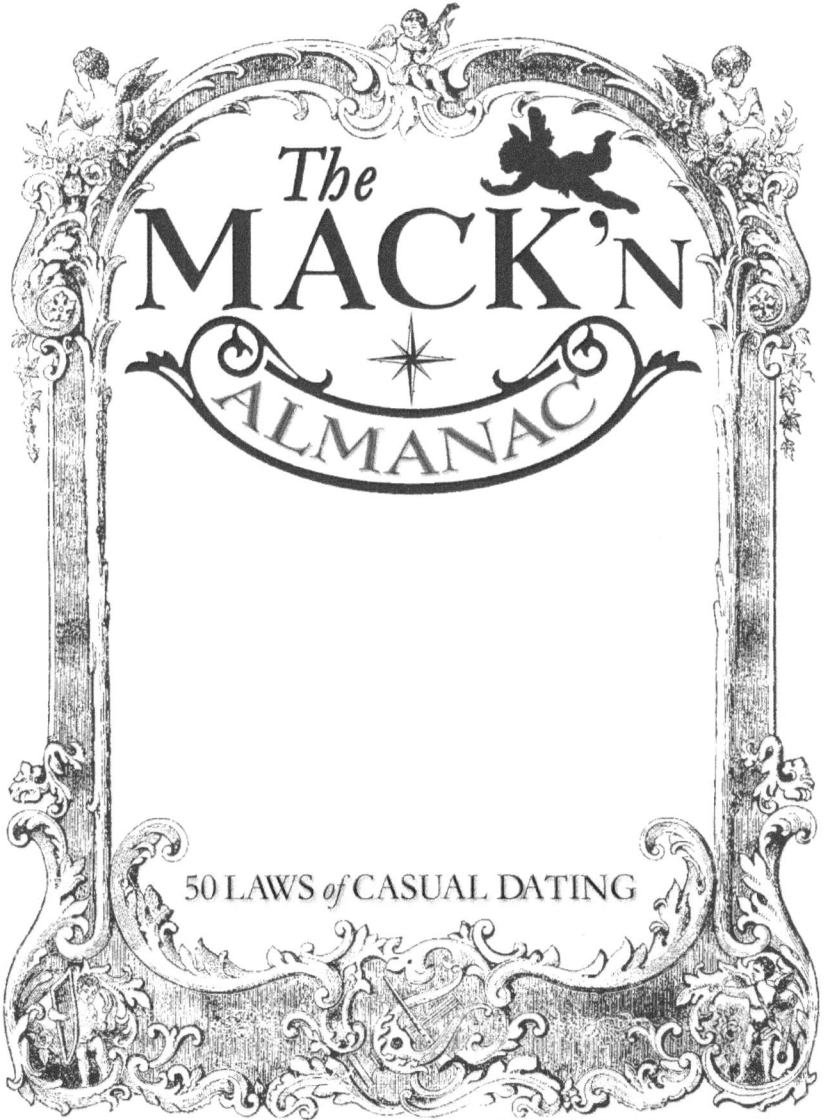

50 LAWS *of* CASUAL DATING

THE OFFICIAL HANDBOOK

by SLICK LEMONS *and* TEZZ WATSON

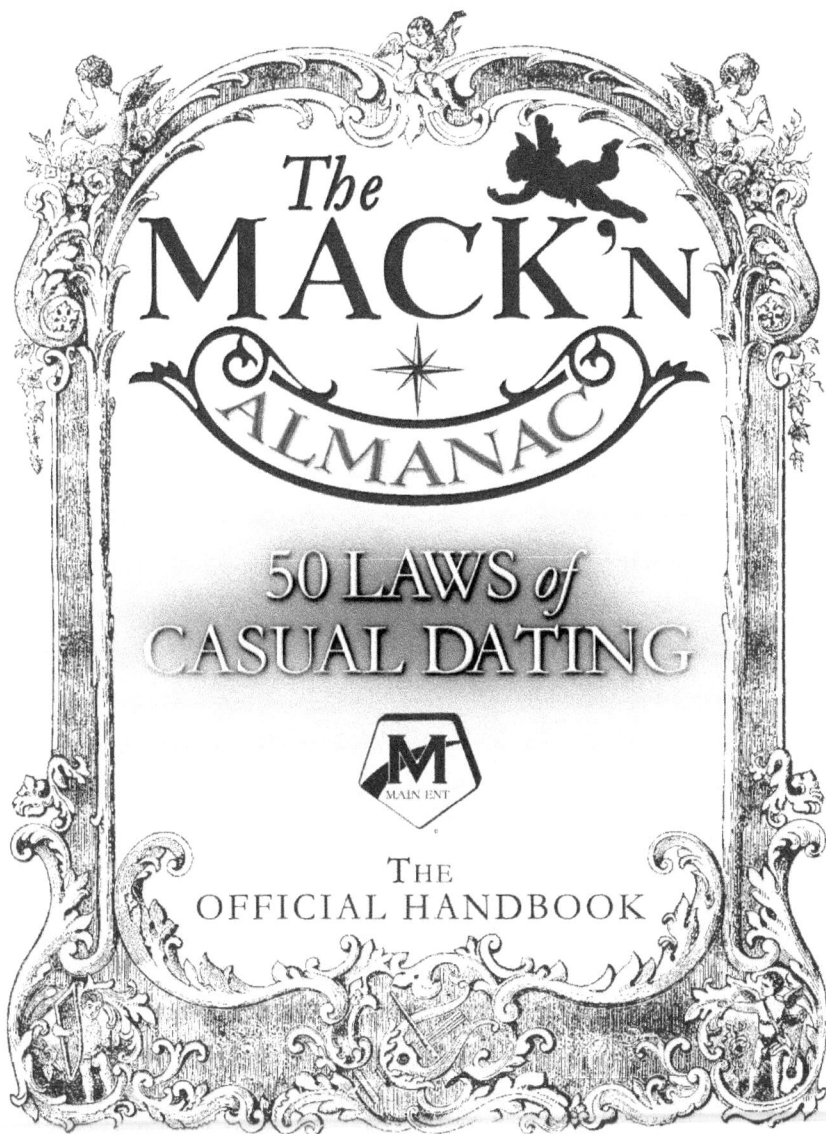

The MACK'N ALMANAC

50 LAWS of CASUAL DATING

M
MAIN ENT

THE OFFICIAL HANDBOOK

by SLICK LEMONS *and* TEZZ WATSON

THE MACK'N ALMANAC
– 50 Laws of Casual Dating *(The Official Handbook)*

First Edition – September 2017

Published by:

M.A.I.N. ENTERTAINMENT, LLC.
www.MainEnt.co

ISBN: 978-0-692-94020-4

Library of Congress Cataloging-in-Publication Data

Category: Self-Help, Casual Dating, Interpersonal Relations, Social Skills, Relationships, Love & Romance

Written by: Slick Lemons

Written by: Tezz Watson

Edited by: Angela Judge | Judge Development Group of Florida, Inc. | JudgeDevelopmentGrp@gmail.com

Cover Designed and Publishing Preparation by: Eli Blyden | www.EliTheBookGuy.com

Printed in the United States of America by: A&A Printing | www.PrintShopCentral.com

Disclaimer

Limit of Liability/Disclaimer of Warranty: While the publisher and author have used their best efforts in preparing this book, they make no representations or warranties with respect to the accuracy or completeness of the contents of this book and specifically disclaim any implied warranties of merchantability or fitness for a particular purpose. No warranty may be created or extended by sales representatives or written sales materials. The advice and strategies contained herein may not be suitable for your situation. You should consult with a professional where appropriate. Neither the publisher nor the author shall be liable for damages arising herefrom.

Dedication

This book is dedicated to
all of the men who are trying to understand women more.
We write this book to give you an advantage in the casual
dating world.

The struggle is real but you can survive.....

Acknowledgement

We stop purposely to thank our families and friends who continue to support us throughout this process and on this continued journey.

We thank all of the seasoned macks on whose shoulders we stand. These are the men who have, in their own way, taught us what to do and what not to do. These are the men who sit on the corners in our neighborhoods, who talk trash but teach lessons. These are the men we listen to even when we weren't supposed to even hang around them.

We thank all of the women for the past experiences we've lived and learned through. Not all of the experiences were good, but we have gained enough from those to pass this information on to the young men coming behind us.

I would like to thank my father and grandfather for passing down the natural gift and ability to communicate with women.

~ Slick

I would like to thank all of the men and women who allowed me to grow, to become my own man. I am grateful for the experiences and the interactions that allowed me to be confident and charismatic.

~ Tezz

We thank the professionals who have guided us through this writing, printing and publishing process.

Table of Contents

Part One:

UNLOCK THE SWAG

Part Two
UNLEASHING THE MACK

Part Three

UNDERSTANDING THE GAME

BONUS INFORMATION

Introduction

The urban dictionary defines a *mack* as a man who is smooth, slick, the best of the best, a pimp, a ladies' man, and a guy who runs everything, a.k.a. the boss. Also as being a man who is always flirting and hitting on women and almost always successful at it too. We somewhat agree with these definitions, but our personal definition for a mack goes a little deeper than that.

We define a *mack* as a man who uses his mind and particular skills to manipulate or control women for his personal benefit. He has the ability to make a woman feel like she's on a pedestal and make her feel on top of the world without actually doing anything or losing control of the situation. He makes her fall in love with his words and personality before his actions.

We never meant for this to be a relationship book because we're not relationship experts. This book isn't meant for any man in a relationship or seeking one. It's not meant for a man looking for love or who's in love with someone because the moment you fall in love with her the laws won't work or apply.

This book is more for the dating man. This book is for the guy who doesn't understand women. He is frozen to the point where he can't even approach women, and if he mustered up enough courage to approach them; he wouldn't even know how to converse with them.

This book is for the guy who just got out of a long exhausting relationship and forgot how to test the waters or date, so to speak. It is for the guy who is tired of being taken advantage of by women and he wants to turn the tables.

This book is comprised of information that we have researched stemming from old macks, retired macks, current macks and from our personal experiences. The laws in this book will transform your dating life as you know it. It will give you the words to say and actions to take when dealing with women.

The laws in this book will have women cater to your every whim without you really giving up little to anything. If you study these laws and apply them to your dating life you will be transformed into a *mack*.

PART ONE:

Unlock the Swag

LAW 1

Never Get Caught Mack'n in Denial

Some guys never come to the realization that they aren't really ladies men. They go out in society not knowing what to do or say when it comes to women, but continue to do what's not working for them. You're mack'n in denial when you repeatedly have intentions on meeting women when you go out, but you reach no results.

This type of guy always has an excuse why he couldn't get a number or any play from women. He's always blaming the women. To avoid being this guy you have to first be real with yourself and realize a change has to take place. Constantly change your approach if you find yourself not getting any play.

Your approach could be your talk-game, appearance, or swag. Sometimes you have to go backwards to move forward, meaning self-reflection; figuring out what you could be doing wrong. The beginning of *The Mack'n Almanac* calls for self-improvement before even stepping to a woman. As you move forward in becoming a full-fledged *mack*, if something isn't working there's nothing wrong with having to go back and taking another look at where you are in the process and making a course correction.

Some men have to refine their tools after being out of the casual dating game for a while, so don't wallow in denial always thinking that it's the women with the problem. Some men need a jumpstart to get going and some men simply have to reboot their game. Whichever situation you find yourself in at this point, you have picked up the right book. Let's get going.

Notes:

_____

_____

_____

_____

_____

_____

_____

_____

_____

LAW 2

Work On Your Flaws

We all have flaws regarding our appearance or personality that we may be insecure about and wish to work on. A man that is able to look in the mirror and identify his flaws takes a step forward in the world of *mack'n*.

To acknowledge that there may be flaws in your personality or appearance, and there is room for improvement is being real with yourself. Prime example, if you feel weight is holding you down from attracting the women you want, join a gym and start a healthy diet.

Another example, we personally have a friend with a receding hairline and for years he's worn hats in public being insecure about it. We convinced him to cut his hair bald and he's been stress free ever since. He gets a lot of attention from more mature and sophisticated women than the young immature type of women that he was used to.

Sometimes it takes switching up your style because that could be a flaw that may be holding you back. Flaws aren't just limited to the physical appearance; you may have to improve your personality.

You may be that man that turns every positive into a negative. Women don't like this type of man because everything turns into a debate. You make her feel like she's stepping on egg shells every time she speaks and you're no fun. If that's you, experience more humor and all the joys that life has to offer so that you can share them with her. It isn't raining every damn day.

You may be that man too goofy that makes her feel like she can't have an intelligent conversation with you without you cracking jokes all the time. She'll feel you have no substance. If this is you, read and become aware of real issues that are going on in the world. Try to enlighten her. Intelligence is very attractive to some women.

This will not happen overnight. Everybody isn't born with everything. It takes time to develop with repetition either it be your personality or your appearance.

Notes:

_____

_____

_____

_____

LAW 3

Take Advantage of Your Strengths

As you are working on your flaws, be sure to take advantage of your strengths and enhance your qualities. Taking advantage of your strengths takes the attention away from your flaws that you are continuously working to improve. Enhancing your qualities makes you stand out more from other guys fighting for a woman's attention.

Most guys that may not be that attractive, or have the best physique make that up in other ways; such as, being a great dresser, having a good sense of humor, intelligent, charming, confident, etc. Some of the least attractive guys with limited funds still get some of the most beautiful women by just using their strengths to hide their weaknesses. As men, we all have specific traits or qualities that make us different. One of the most important things you need to know as a potential *mack* is that you *must* stand out among the rest of the competition by enhancing your qualities.

The way that you stand out is by turning on and off that specific quality that every woman can't resist about you; we call it the *switch mechanism*. It is up to you to discover your own *switch mechanism*. Just like you pre-game before you go out to the club with your friends, have a pre-game approach when it comes to women. It's preparing to showcase your best qualities and strong suits upon engaging in conversation with a woman.

For example, if you are the romantic type of guy approach her with a rose; or if you're the funny type make it your business to bring a smile to her face. Once you grasp her attention keep impressing her by staying consistent with your best qualities because you're the fresh face in her life.

Notes:

_____

_____

_____

_____

_____

_____

_____

_____

LAW 4

Have A Mental Script

Most men have trouble with the opening lines when approaching beautiful women. Some men start to stutter, fumbling over their words, make the dumbest comments, or even their minds go completely blank.

A true *mack* improvises and adjusts his opening lines to the different women he meets; but until you master the art of improvising a mental script is beneficial. Your mental script should be something broad or universal that could apply to all types of women that could break the ice.

Your mental script should consist of you complimenting her and making her laugh at the same time. Once the ice is broken then you ease into improvising. You direct your lines toward her specifically. You will know if your mental script works when you have captured her attention and she is engaging in conversation with you.

If that script worked on her, then that's the script for you. Use it at will, until you feel comfortable enough to take it up a notch and improvise.

Notes:

LAW 5

Develop Your Own Sense of Style

Part of setting yourself apart from other guys is developing your own style or swag.

Everything you wear doesn't have to be name brand or what everyone else has on. It's not always what you have on: it's how you wear it. If you didn't get it by now, we're telling you to develop your own signature look! You need a look that she'll associate with you and even connect it to the time and place where she met you. You want her to remember you.

Don't conform to what the majority is wearing: for example, why stand in a long line in the wee hours of the morning for a pair of Jordan shoes that everyone else will have on? You'll look basically like the typical guy she's used to seeing. Also, when she looks at your True Religion jeans and Jordan shoes she could be tallying up how much you spent and be more interested in your money than getting to know you.

The most important thing to be is clean from head to toe in whatever you have on. When you have swag, a woman can't tell how much money you may have just by looking at you.

In addition to having your signature look, you have to attract her with your fragrance. A woman loves a great smelling man. She'll try to get close to you every chance she gets. After leaving her, it'll be like you're still in her presence with long lasting cologne that she could never get enough of. You'll be heavy on her mind.

Notes:

_____

_____

_____

_____

_____

_____

_____

_____

_____

LAW 6

Be Confident, Not Conceited

Women love a confident man. They can't stand a conceited man. The confident man is a quick thinker. He has witty comebacks or rebuttals for everything she says to him that will make her smile or think.

The conceited man is constantly talking about himself without any regard for her opinion or ideas. He looks in the mirror and takes more pictures of himself than she does.

Being a confident man is being sure of yourself; and not second guessing what to do or say to her. Having confidence makes her feel like you're a big deal and makes her step her game up.

The conceited man is so in to himself he misses any signals from women. Signals that could come from things she says or even does that could be beneficial to him. He speaks so much about himself she'll feel like her wants or needs doesn't even matter. Anything she says he'll somehow relate it to himself.

The confident man lets the woman speak highly of him. He lets his actions speak confidence not his words. He might be *swagged* out in a nice fit, but won't speak on it. It's not his job to admire what he has on, he lets everyone else do that for him unlike the conceited man who has to speak on what he has on and how fly he is. So, it's your job to build your level of confidence.

Notes:

_____

_____

_____

_____

_____

_____

_____

_____

_____

_____

LAW 7

Have A Sense Of Humor

Make her laugh and smile every chance you get. Everyone has a different type of sense of humor. Once you find out what makes her laugh or smile, go for it. This breaks the ice on dates, and dull moments.

There should never be a dull moment when you are around her. It also takes the attention away from you making her mad. You never know what she may be going through in her life, or during the course of a day, and she may need that laugh. She'll appreciate you for it. Be sure as you make her laugh, to reiterate that you are interested in her on other levels.

You don't want to get caught in that friend zone. You'll be stuck as the "cool ass guy friend who makes her laugh," and nothing more. She will never take you seriously, but only as a joke. No pun intended.

Notes:

_____

_____

_____

_____

_____

_____

_____

_____

_____

_____

_____

_____

_____

_____

_____

LAW 8

Be Versatile

It doesn't take for you to have a degree to impress her with topics or a subject you can speak intelligently on.

A *mack* should be well rounded and should educate himself on all subjects that would impress a woman. If you have traveled, impress her with all of the places you've been and things you've done there. If you're a handyman, tell her something that might benefit her regarding her car or home repairs. If you're a food connoisseur, let her know all the places that have the best type of food she likes and describe it to her.

Also be in touch with the current entertainment, local, and world news. The average woman doesn't expect a guy to hold an intelligent conversation. Also absolutely do not speak on anything you don't know about. You don't want to sound like a fool.

Notes:

_____

_____

_____

_____

_____

_____

_____

_____

_____

_____

_____

_____

_____

_____

_____

_____

LAW 9

Be Honest

The last thing you want to be is labeled as a liar. A woman's trust is golden. It's hard to gain it or even keep it considering the fact that the majority of women have trust issues anyway from dealing with dishonest exes.

Guys lie over the dumbest things even when we don't even have to. Sometimes we even volunteer lies. Make yourself an open book to her if she asks questions. Make it seem it like you have nothing to hide. When you are dating, there is no reason to lie because you two aren't obligated to each other.

Let her know you are an outgoing person and that you are entertaining other women. Let her know you like to go different places and that you enjoy good company. You are basically telling her you are casual dating and that you are not exclusive with anyone. This tells her that you have other options.

The reason that you are telling her this is so that she could never bring this up to you as an issue. You were honest about yourself in the beginning, which gave her a choice to leave you alone or proceed to get to know you. The majority of women proceed because they think that they can change a man, but in actuality we change for who we want when we want.

When you tell her the truth she'll respect you more. Tell her that you care for her and that's why you tell her the truth. Also being honest doesn't require you to tell her everything. Some things aren't any of her business and you might have to check her on personal matters that may not be any of her concern.

Notes:

_____

_____

_____

_____

_____

_____

_____

_____

_____

PART TWO

Unleashing the Mack

LAW 10

Be Patient

I know when you first meet a beautiful woman, and you exchange numbers you can get overzealous sometimes. Man, just be patient and chill. Let her come to you and give her the same attention she gives you. Don't blow her phone up or constantly try to see her because you'll be smothering her. She'll think you're thirsty when you sweat her like that.

The willingness to get to know each other has to be mutual. When you are not patient, you tend to rush and make mistakes. When you're not patient, you aren't thinking and she could take advantage of you.

If you're so blinded by her beauty, and adamant about rushing into something, she could easily flip the script on you. You could find yourself spending more money than time. She'll call you when she wants something instead of wanting you. And when she calls, you'll give her anything in hopes of spending time with her.

All the signs were there in the beginning, if you would've been patient and just took the time to get to know her, you would still be in control.

Notes:

_____

_____

_____

_____

_____

_____

_____

_____

_____

_____

_____

LAW 11

Never Settle For Less

In a social setting, never settle for less than what you really want. Try to talk to women you want and not settle for the women that may be an easy *yes*.

Don't be intimidated by a woman's beauty and settle for a less attractive choice because you are afraid of rejection. Go for who you really want. Most beautiful women are down to earth, but the average man isn't brave enough to talk to her because he doesn't think he has a chance, or doesn't know how to approach her.

You only live once so why settle for less than what you really want. Value yourself and she'll see the value in you, too. Have confidence and approach women to whom you are absolutely attracted to. We live by the rule that it is better to be rejected by someone we found very attractive than to be rejected by someone we were just settling for.

Notes:

LAW 12

Groups:
The Roles Your Partners Play

When a group of guys are entertaining ladies within a group setting there should always be role players. A lot of guys make the mistake in being in competition hindering each other from making any progress with the group of ladies.

Each guy has a role to play helping the next man out; you have *the conversationalist, the comedian, the eye candy,* and *the hero*.

THE CONVERSATIONALIST is the guy who engages in lively conversation with all of the ladies. He keeps all of their attention on the group of guys. He constantly brings up relevant and irrelevant topics keeping things interesting. He breaks the ice and keeps conversation flowing so there isn't a dull moment. His job is to keep you from hearing the crickets so to speak.

THE COMEDIAN is the guy that keeps the ladies laughing and having a good time. His job is to not let things get too serious within the group and help the ladies relax. He gets the ladies defenses down and makes them feel comfortable enough to come out of their shell. He might crack a joke or two at the expense of someone else, but it's nothing personal. He works well assisting the Conversationalist.

THE EYE CANDY is labeled as the most attractive out of the group to the women. He grasps their attention off of his looks alone so he doesn't have to speak much. When he does speak he's very charming and persuasive, which helps to entice the women to come even more out of their shells; for example a woman that doesn't normally drink he could have her taking shots. The comedian may crack jokes at his expense, but he doesn't take it personal; it only brings him more attention.

THE HERO may be the most important of the roles. You know that there is an unattractive annoying cock-blocking woman in every group who never wants to see her friends enjoying themselves. This woman bugs her friends to leave early because nobody is paying her any attention.

Well the Hero has to take on the task of entertaining her, so she won't sabotage the whole get-together. We guys call it taking one for the team. If she's happy then the rest of her squad is happy. The Hero prevents her from intervening in one-on-one conversations, hating on the other men, and prevents her from getting the women to leave early.

Notes:

_____

_____

_____

_____

_____

_____

_____

_____

_____

_____

_____

_____

_____

_____

_____

_____

LAW 13

Win Her with the First Impression

Now, when you see an attractive woman in public, win her with a strong positive first impression: win her with some game.

Before approaching her analyze her actions, surroundings, and appearance. Use all of these to help initiate a conversation. While approaching her, greet her making eye contact with your hand extended; state your name, and ask for hers. Compliment her attire or any physical appearance you find attractive immediately. Make small talk with her incorporating humor into the conversation. Compliment her on something regarding her personality that sticks out that you like. Then use this quote exactly or in your own words: *"You seem like a cool person. I would like to get to know you further. Please tell me you're not spoken for."*

Eighty percent of the time you will get her number regardless if she is in a relationship or not. The other 20% of the time she's in a committed relationship and she's not cheating or you aren't her type.

Notes:

LAW 14

A Two Drink Maximum

Whenever you are initiating contact with a woman, you have to remember to limit yourself to having only two (2) drinks at the most. A lot of men use liquid courage when first trying to initiate a conversation with a woman. Alcohol may relax you. Drinking may help you not to over think, which seems to increase your confidence, or for the moment when you are a little tipsy, you may not care about getting turned down.

That's all good I guess, but when you become inebriated that's a problem. A man should have no more than two drinks when trying to spark a conversation with a woman. With two drinks you should feel relaxed, but still sharp, and the words should flow like a river when talking to her.

You should have an answer or comeback for anything she throws your way. If you're drunk, you become sloppy and your thought process is impaired.

You also want to remember important things that she shares with you to bring up in another conversation which shows her that you listen to her. If you're drunk, you won't remember half the conversation.

Notes:

_____

_____

_____

_____

_____

_____

_____

_____

_____

_____

_____

_____

LAW 15

Have an Exit Strategy

Believe it or not women do this all the time. Before going out on a date or simply just chilling with a woman for the first time, notify one of your friends to give you a call around a specific time.

Instruct your friend to call you twice. The first phone call is to verify if her physical appearance is up to par. Everybody knows that club light with the influence of alcohol could turn a Beast into Beyoncé. So if she is physically unattractive come up with a code word to let him know on the first phone call.

He'll keep calling back to back thus requiring you to leave due to a sudden emergency. If she is attractive give him a code word letting him know everything is fine physically. The second phone call is to verify if the vibe is right between you two. She might say or do something that may turn you totally off. Everybody has their instant deal breakers; For example, smoking cigarettes is a deal breaker for both of us.

Once again repeat the same process with the code word giving him a Yea or Nay. Your night either would end early or late spending it with a new acquaintance.

Notes:

_____

_____

_____

_____

_____

_____

_____

_____

_____

_____

_____

_____

LAW 16

Construct A Roster

If you're dating or know that you are going to date more than one woman, then you will need to categorize them according by your chemistry with them, their appearance, intelligence, etc. Think of it as developing a professional sports team. You have your first, second, and third string.

FIRST STRING LADIES are the women you could picture yourself being in a relationship with even though you're not in one or pursuing a relationship. She has all the qualities you would want in a girlfriend. She gets the red carpet treatment from you, meaning frequent and longer conversations on the phone. They get to be seen with you in public places where you wouldn't mind being seen by anybody.

SECOND STRING LADIES are women who you get along with to a certain extent, but not as much as your first string. Your conversations consist of texts more so than talking. You don't go many places with her in public but when you do go, be very aware of your surroundings because you don't want to jeopardize your first string spot.

The second string can't move up because she has something about her that you just can't get over for her to be a first string. It may be something about her physical appearance or even her personality.

THIRD STRING LADIES are women that you only have to do the bare minimum to keep them satisfied on your team, so that's why they get the bare minimum from you. They don't ask for much other than time. The time you give them is at night mostly or after the club.

They enjoy watching bootlegs, movies and shows on Firestick, Netflix, and eating fast food. They are real homebodies. They just want you to be there all the time, but they'll take what they can get. You have contact with her strictly by text.

If you accurately utilize these principles, this law lets you know that it's possible to have more than one woman in each category.

Notes:

_____

_____

_____

_____

LAW 17

Prioritize Your Time with Any Woman

The previous law in *The Mack'n Almanac* demonstrated the importance of constructing a roster but this law helps you understand how that roster will help you make the best choices with your time.

Of course your time will be limited between business and pleasure. By pleasure I mean quality time with your roster of women. Time should be divided according to level of importance of your roster.

First string ladies should get the majority of your attention and time. Wine and dine them once in a while, but don't spoil them too much with your time. Remember neither of these ladies is your girlfriend, they are just first string on your team.

Second string ladies get time left over from the first string. You should have second string ladies ready and willing to spend time with you when your first string ladies are unavailable, or when you are on bad terms with the first string ladies.

A third string lady only gets the bare minimum. She gets the late night creep treatment: she's the one to call after the club when neither the first string nor second string ladies are answering the phone. A third stringer is just your *fallback female* who is thirsty for your attention and companionship.

*** *Bonus Alert* ***

There are at least 10 different types of Women that we have met on our journey. Check out how we have identified them.

Notes:

_____

_____

_____

_____

_____

_____

_____

_____

LAW 18

Make Your Standards Known

From the jump, you have got to set the standard. You must let her know that there are some things that you just won't tolerate. Let her know off rip that there are things she could do that would get her fired instantly.

Every man has their own list of things but some may consist of going through your phone, popping up to your crib without calling, or constantly asking where you are or what are you doing just to keep tabs on you. Most women try to play it cool and act like they don't do those list of things, but we know when women get emotional they're liable to do just about anything.

Also a way you could tell that a woman is feeling you is if after you let her know of your standards, you see that she is going out of her way to meet them. It's like a bar you set that they're trying to reach by doing your likes and avoiding your dislikes.

Letting your standards known in the beginning could also make it easier for you to get out of a situation you don't want to be in as well. When she does something you told her you didn't like from the jump, she can only be mad at herself when you let her go.

Make your pet peeves known in the BEGINNING, so you won't have to deal with them in the END.

Notes:

_____

_____

_____

_____

_____

_____

_____

_____

_____

_____

_____

LAW 19

Remember To Do The Small Things

Always behave like a gentleman when dating. The small things matter most to a woman. Remember to open doors, to pull out her chair, let her walk in front of you, and most importantly stay off your phone.

Make her your priority from start to finish. She should have your undivided attention when you're spending time with her. Show her that it's all about her while also staying true to the *mack* you are.

Every woman has her own little nuances, things that turn her on, shit that they like for a man to do. Flattery is a must. Do the small things that bring her instant gratification, making her feel special, and unique in her own way: you don't want her to feel like she's just the next one in your long line of conquests, even though she might be, your goal is to make sure she doesn't feel like it.

The things we are mentioning might seem small, but they will really stand out in her eyes and will leave a lasting impression. She may not remember how much you spent, but she'll damn sure remember how you treated her on a date.

Some women will just come out and tell you, but with others you might have to do a little work to find out what are the small things to which she will respond. If you pay attention to the details, you'll easily find out what excites her and how to get a positive response from her.

When you remember the small things, she recognizes that you're taking an interest by learning her do's and don'ts. Once you find out the small things do them at will, and she'll appreciate you for that.

Notes:

_____

_____

_____

_____

_____

_____

_____

_____

LAW 20

Spending Money on Her

A real *mack* must be very careful on how and why you spend money on her. You don't want to get caught in a money trap, meaning putting money into her without anything in return. You don't want to be the guy who's just paying someone for her attention.

You also don't want to be seen as an investor. You could find yourself paying her monthly bills, buying clothes, shoes, purses, paying for hairdos, cosigning for a car etc. But what is the return on this kind of investment? All of that was done for her, and none of it is benefiting you at all.

When I say benefits I'm suggesting anything you may want out of a woman such as, time, attention, conversation, moral support, financial freedom, desire, or even affection. Don't ever put more money or let alone anything into a woman than you are getting back. That would be a bad investment.

Make it known in the beginning that you love an independent woman. Once you have established that in the beginning, she won't always be coming to you with her hand out. Tell her that you like nice things, but you are not a materialistic person. Instead of possessions that lose their value, you more so value experiences because those memories are priceless.

Explain to her in the beginning that you rather spend your money getting to know her by taking her places and doing things she has never experienced before.

Notes:

_____

_____

_____

_____

_____

_____

_____

_____

_____

_____

LAW 21

MACK'N VS. Trick'n

A lot of guys get *mack'n* and *trick'n* misunderstood and can't tell the difference. They will think that they are *mack'n* when they are really *trick'n*. Macks lead with their minds and guys that trick lead with their money.

A *mack* reaps all of the benefits from a woman for free that a guy who *tricks* has to pay for. When *macks* choose to spend money it is always beneficial to them, and what they spend money on always consists in something interactive. A guy that *tricks* never gives a woman a chance to know him. He only gives her a chance to know his money. He's that guy at the club continuously buying a woman drinks to get her number only for her not even to remember him when he calls or texts.

The time that the tricking guy spends with a woman consists of anything that benefits her such as shopping sprees at the mall, getting her nails/feet done, getting her hair done, paying her bills, etc. This type of guy has no talk-game, swag, or personality about him. If he does he doesn't know how to use it. Women tend to take advantage of this guy and I don't blame them.

Notes:

_____

_____

_____

_____

_____

_____

_____

_____

_____

_____

_____

_____

LAW 22

Never Argue or Fight Over A Woman

Some men are willing to argue and fight over women that aren't even theirs. Instead of stepping their game up, they want to emasculate other men in hopes of winning over women. They lack all of the abilities and skills to keep a woman's undivided attention, so they get confrontational with everyone else she is interacting with.

As a *mack* you should never entertain this behavior. Your value depreciates when you feed this type of attention. Time is worth more than anything and the fact that a woman chooses to spend her time with you over anybody else says a lot. While the other guy is trying to bait you into entertaining his ignorance you're getting the best of him entertaining her.

By constantly going back and forth with him on social media, publicly, or by phone you draw the attention away from the woman losing sight of your main objective which is her. She'll be fed up with the both of you leaving you both alone.

Also another reason you don't argue or fight over a woman is that it'll make you look bad if she isn't the best in quality. For example she may be your third stringer meaning little to anything to you, but she is his everything. It makes you look bad to be getting into unnecessary drama over a woman that you see only late nights to every blue moon. Your reputation can be at stake and if that's what it comes down to then leave her alone.

Notes:

_____

_____

_____

_____

_____

_____

_____

_____

_____

LAW 23

Be Original

If a woman is single, you better believe she's entertaining other guys. Your job is to make yourself stand out from those other guys. Your whole demeanor has to be different from them. Make her remember you every time you spend time with her.

Leave a lasting impression. Think of other things to do other than the usual dinner and a movie for example museums, wine tasting, festivals, tours, etc. When you do take her to a movie, make it CINEBISTRO instead of AMC or MUVICO. Cinebistro is a smaller and more intimate environment: the more exclusive the location, the better. These small steps will set you apart from other guys.

If you're dining out get on www.Zomato.com and look up a place she's never been before. Also Groupon is a great inexpensive way to do out of the ordinary things on a date. I personally had an exclusive low key spot way out at a beach that I used to take selective women to. It was never crowded, very clean, and it was somewhere they have never been. If you catch the sunset just right, it'll trump any amount of money spent on a dinner or movie. Originality is a major key. This law keeps you two steps ahead of the rest.

Notes:

_____

_____

_____

_____

_____

_____

_____

_____

_____

_____

_____

_____

Be Unpredictable –
Do Not Have A Routine

The last thing you want her to do is figure out your way of thinking, your schedule outside of work, your actions, and the things you say.

You're supposed to know her better than she knows you. Don't designate specific days or times to *cake up* or have a specific date night. She'll expect this from you all of the damn time.

When you are constantly calling her at a certain time, hanging with her on certain days, or even texting her a "hey beautiful" all the damn time, you are setting a standard. Now there is nothing wrong with this standard that you are setting if you are trying to get serious with her; but in the realm of casual dating things aren't that serious.

This standard of treatment that you are setting for yourself will be expected upon you from her all of the time. It becomes routine. Something she'll get used to. It'll drive you insane casually dating different women trying to keep up a routine for each one.

The best routine is to have no routine and be spontaneous. It also keeps things exciting and interesting. She won't know what to expect from you. This law keeps you in control of the situation.

Notes:

_____

_____

_____

_____

_____

_____

_____

_____

_____

_____

_____

LAW 25

Listen To Her and Ask Questions

Women love to talk - period. If they feel comfortable enough around you, they'll tell you their life story as soon as they meet you. As hard as it may be, your job is to listen, and remember every little detail they tell you.

Ask questions and look her in her eyes to show that you're intrigued by her and eager to learn more about her. You will learn about past relationships, her family, her likes and dislikes, her turn-ons and turn-offs, her favorite movies, her favorite foods, etc. Treat this like a study guide and take mental notes because she's basically giving you the answers to her test.

You won't have to work hard at all to get to know her because she's telling you who she is all at once. You will use this to your advantage to win her over. When she tries to figure you out and get to know you, don't give her too much. Give her an answer, but spoon feed her little by little at a time on who you are. Try to keep the focus on her by repeatedly asking her questions about her life, and then she'll give you long elaborate answers. This law allows you to find out what she wants in a man faster than you could naturally.

Notes:

_____

_____

_____

_____

_____

_____

_____

_____

_____

_____

_____

LAW 26

Women Lie; Men Lie

When you meet a woman don't be a fool. Just like men, they can put on a front to make themselves seem like the perfect candidate for you.

When you first meet a woman, you're really getting to know her "representative." She is not showing you her true self. There is always more to the woman you meet at first...there is always more to her story. Things are *not always* the way she will make it seem. Some women make you believe that they have it more together than they really do. Digging a little deeper, asking the right questions will let you find out more of the "real" story than the woman may tell you at first.

It's exactly like the makeup they wear. Women put all of this makeup on their faces to mask and hide the imperfections on it. Well, the same thing is applied to their lives when you first meet a woman, but eventually the makeup has to come off. Eventually, the truth will come out and you will meet the real woman behind her mask.

Women will sell you a façade and it's a lot easier nowadays because of social media/text messaging. When getting to know a woman you want to have the upper hand by having face to face conversations, digging deep, and moving off of facts instead of hearsay.

Notes:

_____

_____

_____

_____

_____

_____

_____

_____

_____

_____

LAW 27

Pay Attention to Details

We cannot stress enough for you to pay attention to details when you visit a woman's home. The way a woman takes care of her home can speak a lot about how she takes care of herself meaning personal hygiene.

We know it sounds crazy, but if a woman's cleanliness is as important to you as it is to us, then you will check the status of her bathroom, kitchen, and bedroom.

Some women don't treat being clean as a lifestyle. Some only treat it as a requirement when looking their best to go to the club. Pay attention to details within her home when visiting.

If her home isn't up to par even after she's invited you over, then that's a red flag to the fact that she may not be very clean. She had more than enough time to prepare. Looks aren't everything fellas when it comes to a clean woman.

Notes:

_____

_____

_____

_____

_____

_____

_____

_____

_____

_____

_____

_____

_____

_____

_____

LAW 28

Have Self-Restraint

We stress that for the first time when you are alone with her in a private setting that you exercise self-restraint. This is one of the hardest rules for a man to follow, let alone a *mack*. Women will test you by chilling with you in a private setting on the first occasion to see where your mind is.

Your prime objective is to stay reserved and resist her no matter how much she flirts with you or tries to tempt you sexually. She might wear short seductive clothing, lay all up on you while watching TV or a movie, talk about what she likes done to her sexually, and touch you certain places on the sly.

If anything, flirt with her back and get her aroused to make her feel the same way she's making you feel, but keep your composure. Now there are exceptions to this rule. If she is aggressive to the point to where she's basically attempting to take your clothes off or if she's taking her own clothes off, throw this rule out the window and go for yours.

Just know a woman is way more turned on by you not giving in to her on the first time chilling with her. If you don't give in to her, you could get more out of her in the long run. She'll think you're not all about sex and that you respect her. DON'T DO WHAT SHE EXPECTS YOU TO DO, DO THE UNEXPECTED.

Notes:

_____

_____

_____

_____

_____

_____

_____

_____

_____

_____

LAW 29

Be Careful With Your Conversations

Another very important thing to remember is for you to shy away for the *"who you know"* or *"what high school did you attend"* kind of conversations. Although it makes for easy conversation, you have to avoid these two topics when you first meet a woman. There is more of a chance that the outcome of the conversation will not be beneficial to you and your plans for this young lady.

If you get into playing the name game, and find that you have been involved with one of her friends, or even one of her enemies, it can disqualify you instantly. It's better for her to find out about such involvements after she has gained deep feelings for you. Only inquire about her family to make sure you're nowhere down the line related to each other.

Also stay away from conversations about high school. If you're constantly talking about high school or the past, it shows her you haven't grown up much and you have a lot of growing up to do. It's better to live in the present and tell her your future plans in life.

Notes:

_____

_____

_____

_____

_____

_____

_____

_____

_____

_____

_____

_____

_____

_____

_____

_____

LAW 30

Let Her Know
You Have Goals and Plans

Women tend to measure if a man is worth their time by what he has done in his life, what he is doing now with his life, and what he plans on doing in the future. You may not be where you want to be in your life, but as long as you are working toward it you'll be fine. Just make sure you are financially stable while working toward it.

Make her see that there is substance to you and that you aren't just a bum that doesn't want anything out of life. Once you tell her your goals, she'll respect you and give you the time that it may require to take the steps in achieving them. If you are busy working toward that goal, she'll definitely try to support you.

This also helps her understand that your time with her is limited and she can't get upset if you have to leave to handle business.

Notes:

_____

_____

_____

_____

_____

_____

_____

_____

_____

_____

_____

_____

_____

_____

LAW 31

Support and Encourage Her with Her Goals in Life

When you take a personal interest in what is important to her, she will look at you in a new light. A man may have never supported her or encouraged her to follow her passion or achieve her goals. When we mean support, it doesn't necessarily have to mean giving her money.

If she is in school help her study. If she is opening her own business for the first time, help her promote it and get the word out. Give her ideas to help her get started to follow her dreams. Utilize your own connections, if you have any, to help her achieve her goals. This will leave a long lasting impression on her.

The bridges will never burn between you two no matter what because of the support you have shown her, which means you can always go back to her.

Notes:

_____

_____

_____

_____

_____

_____

_____

_____

_____

_____

_____

_____

_____

_____

_____

_____

LAW 32

Read Her Body Language

Fellas, try this: within the course of a deep conversation with a woman or heated argument never lose eye contact with her. Don't look away; engage in her as if you're looking straight through her. In my experience in doing this I've encountered one of these different personalities: The Little Girl, The Immature Teen, or The Grown Ass Woman.

THE LITTLE GIRL is the emotional or sensitive woman that cries because you're forcing them to open up. She feels comfortable with you and she sees the sincerity in your eyes. You might be forcing her to address some issues she has within herself. The way you approach this is by giving her a listening ear while she vents. Help her purge all of the negativity out her system simply by talking to her about them and being sympathetic. This helps you not be the target of deep rooted issues and also understand her behavior better so that you can act accordingly.

THE IMMATURE TEEN is the woman that shies away or avoids eye contact. She's constantly looking away or looking down avoiding the conversation. She doesn't want to address any issues and feels you're talking to her or looking at her as if you're her FATHER. She gets an attitude from you wanting to dig deep and get personal with her.

Slick Lemons: *"Personally had an issue like this with a woman a long time ago. She was acting out in this manner because she developed deep feelings for me and it was eating her up inside knowing our relationship wasn't going to the next level. The way I handled it was by keeping things casual."*

Don't touch on topics that will lead to relationship conversations. Keep things fun and light. Don't discuss anything serious that is related to relationships. She knows how things are between you two, but doesn't like to be reminded of it.

Slick: *"Digging deep with this personality type in a woman could backfire, so I urge you not to do so."*

THE GROWN ASS WOMAN embraces this type of eye contact. She sees it as a challenge willing to take on any conversation and throw it right back to you. Some men can't handle this type of woman. She has quick and witty responses showing no fear. If you ask she surely will tell you straight no chase and be prepared for the same question. You have to be a quick thinker when dealing with this type of woman because she is very experienced. You have to show confidence and no weakness when speaking to this woman. Also have thick skin because she speaks her mind as you should speak yours. She may challenge you in everything and hates being wrong. Sometimes let her have the argument if it's not serious so that you could move on to a subject that could bring you closer to her.

Notes:

_____

_____

_____

_____

_____

_____

_____

_____

_____

_____

_____

_____

LAW 33

Do Not Argue With Her

It's okay to have disagreements, but don't let them escalate into an argument. While she's steady trying to prove a point and win an argument, you focus on compromising the situation saying that you both were wrong.

Give her solutions that could avoid this situation again. Compliment her or make her smile while she's trying to stay mad at you and argue. Once she smiles in the heat of her attempting to argue with you, YOU WON!!

Bring her close, hug and kiss her, and she'll say, *"Move I'm trying to stay mad at you"*, then she'll smile.

THIS LAW WILL LEAD TO SEX 80% OF THE TIME.

Notes:

_____

_____

_____

_____

_____

_____

_____

_____

_____

_____

_____

_____

_____

_____

PART THREE

Understanding the Game

LAW 34

Control Social Media

Nine times out of 10 the women that you're casually dating are your friends on social media. Don't allow social media to create unnecessary drama in your life.

Maintain a low profile by limiting what you share online. You don't have to post what you're doing, where you're eating, and where you're going all day every day. You open the door for women to question you on your activities and keep tabs on you. For example, you might've told her over the phone you were tired and was going to sleep; but the picture of you and your friends posted on your page enjoying yourselves in the strip club says otherwise.

It probably was a last minute decision to go, but that is beside the point. If you wouldn't have put your business out there she wouldn't have known. Now she's in her feelings because she's thinking you didn't want to spend time with her and you lied. Now you have to explain yourself.

Basically leave the constant social media postings to the women and also try to avoid taking pictures with them. This will save you lots of headaches.

Notes:

_____

_____

_____

_____

_____

_____

_____

_____

_____

_____

_____

_____

LAW 35

Befriend One Woman; Catch Five Women

This strategy is a great and proven way to meet women without doing little to nothing.

Build an innocent platonic relationship with a woman of your childhood, coworker, or even someone you went to school with. Make sure the both of you understand that this is just a friendship and nothing more.

Make it your business to be aware of her lady friends and associates. Any time she is around her friends or associates briefly slide through to show your face and allow her to introduce you to everyone. As much as women love to talk, best believe you'll definitely be the topic of conversation once you leave.

When women talk amongst themselves about you it gets them curious. If one of them knows someone you used to date that's even better because they'll be eager to want to know more about you for themselves. You better believe that your female friend will tell them all of your business, but don't get upset; see it as promotion. Women will inquire about you through her and you'll inquire about some women through her as well.

Also whatever you do, don't put your friend in the middle of a situation to where she feels she may have to take a side. Her job is to connect you with other women, not to carry on any he say or she say between you and the women.

Once you connect with the women, the rest is none of her business. The other women shouldn't impact the personal friendship you have with her in anyway.

Notes:

_____

_____

_____

_____

_____

_____

_____

LAW 36

Do Not Overwhelm Yourself

If you feel yourself getting overwhelmed with trying to give time, attention, or affection to too many women it's time to cut the insignificant ones off of your roster altogether. If you followed **LAW 16** on prioritizing your roster and you still feel overwhelmed you have too many first strings or second strings.

You don't have to focus on third strings because there role on your roster is already irrelevant. At this time you have to really compare your first and second strings' qualities. Think about the qualities that are important to you in a woman and who possesses them.

Think about the things you like for your woman to do for you and who is most successful at doing them. Create your own personal test by putting them in a situation and see who deals with it the best. This helps you see who is worth your time and attention.

Notes:

_____

_____

_____

_____

_____

_____

_____

_____

_____

_____

_____

_____

_____

_____

_____

LAW 37

Mack'n in a Workplace Environment

There are some workplace environments that have an abundance of beautiful women. I am referring to corporate office settings, but specifically call center jobs. You will see predominately women working these jobs because it involves constantly talking on the phone which most men don't like to do. The men that are successful in this profession though reap the benefits from the beautiful women of this environment.

Most women who work in this profession spend more time at work than at home, not to mention the occasional overtime she decides to put in. With that being said, the little to no attention her man gives her or having no man at all definitely works out in your favor. The fact that she sees you the majority of time on a daily basis, makes her develop a physical attraction towards you based off of visual and comfort level.

In a workplace setting the best thing a potential Mack should focus on is being patient and playing it cool as possible because all you have is time; 40hrs a week. A few things to remember is always have a positive attitude toward your female coworkers and compliment them on the little things that nobody else may notice.

Complimenting on the little things is a great way to spark up a conversation. The fact that you pay that much attention to her by pointing out things nobody acknowledges will create quite an impression upon her. Also stay attentive when a female coworker is talking to you. This will help you pick up any signs or signals she may be trying to send you telling you she's digging you.

By being able to read her signs or signals you'll definitely know when she's going out of her way to get your attention. As long as you keep calm, play it cool, and stay out of the workplace spotlight the female coworker is most likely to make the first move.

Notes:

_____

_____

_____

_____

_____

_____

LAW 38

Two Women Same Place Same Time

A lot of men have been in the awkward and uncomfortable situation of having two women that they are dating in the same place at the same time.

Most of these situations have gone terribly wrong due to them not knowing how to deal with the situation. This situation mostly can occur at social gatherings such as clubs, birthday parties, family/friend's BBQs, etc.

The first thing to remember in this situation is to not avoid them, but acknowledge them both at different times. If you avoid them they'll sense that you're acting different and something isn't right. By acknowledging them saying hello with a hug, she'll never suspect someone else is there and everything is just as cool as usual.

Another thing to remember is to not give too much of your time to one or the other. Doing this, singles them out. If you repeatedly keep giving specific attention to both women they'll notice each other then they'll start to ask questions inquiring about each other.

Last but not least stay mingling. If you stay mingling it makes it hard for them to keep up with you. Keep moving amongst your family or friends giving them more of your attention making it hard to keep up with you.

Notes:

_____

_____

_____

_____

_____

_____

_____

_____

_____

_____

LAW 39

Dealing with a Woman with Kids

Proceed with caution: Understand the territory that you are entering when dealing with a woman with younger or even older kids. A woman becomes a package deal when she has kids. You can't have one without the other unless her kids are grown and out of the picture. Your objective is to acknowledge and show respect to the whole family without seeming like you're trying to take the place of their father or assume the role of a father.

If a woman wants you to meet her kids, you are a big deal to her. Try prolonging meeting her kids as long as you could. Come through after their bed time and leave before they wake up. Let her know you would like to meet them when you feel comfortable.

When you do meet them have a laid back or cool approach toward them like you're not a threat. Older kids usually mind their own business if you're not trying to be in their business. I would stay away from doing any more than I would have to winning over the acceptance of the kids. They'll get attached to you and in some cases you'll get attached to them.

Notes:

_____

_____

_____

_____

_____

_____

_____

_____

_____

_____

_____

_____

LAW 40

Keep Her Satisfied Sexually

Along with satisfying her mentally and emotionally, you have to satisfy her sexually. Fulfill her every sexual desire. You may not love her at all, but the way you have sex with her will make her think you do.

There is no room for selfishness in the bedroom because this department will ensure she won't be going anywhere. To stimulate her sexually on top of all the other ways that you already do, will make you the total package for her. Specifically, slowly pleasure her at first to make her feel like its loving making. Then get a bit rough while gripping certain parts of her body. Put her and lock her in different positions. Please her orally slowly hitting her spot so that she can't resist.

If you do as many things that she will allow you to do to her, you will cover all bases. Leave no stone unturned. Also you must evaluate her sex game to see if it's up to par. You must see if she can satisfy you and that she isn't selfish in the bedroom. If you can complete this rule successfully, you can get a lot from her and get away with a lot more when dealing with her. Also be selective on who gets what treatment: *every woman **doesn't** deserve the oral treatment.*

Notes:

_____

_____

_____

_____

_____

_____

_____

_____

_____

_____

_____

LAW 41

Live A Magnum Lifestyle

There is nothing wrong with sowing your royal oats when dating a variety of different women, but there is a problem with not protecting yourself.

By all means please protect yourself. Stay strapped with condoms in all of your pants pockets, car, under your bed, couch, kitchen, bathroom, etc. Trust us, it can go down wherever.

Doing this minimizes the chances of you being "up in the moment" or getting caught slipping with "drunk sex". Just as some guys trap women, some women will do the same. These are some of the things some women may use to avoid having you use protection, just know that she probably has a hidden agenda when you hear: *"I'm on birth control," "I just wanna feel you inside of me," "It dries me out," "I'm in A-1 health," "I don't think I can have kids," or "I'm allergic to rubbers."*

Some women will even try to flip the script and accuse you of having sex with other women as your reasoning behind always wanting use protection with them. It's almost like they're trying to bait you into not using it.

Explain to them you live a *"Magnum Lifestyle"* and you just prefer to be safe rather than sorry.

Notes:

_____

_____

_____

_____

_____

_____

_____

_____

_____

_____

LAW 42

No Extended Stays

Do not sleep over her house or allow her to sleep over yours past one night. This is the quickest way for a woman to get too attached and too comfortable.

Sleeping over each other's places past one night creates a relationship environment that you don't want. If you are up under each other all day and night for some days straight, it creates that relationship seed in her mind about how things could be.

This relationship seed will continue to grow more rapid than usual with these sleepovers exceeding one night. She starts getting used to coming home to you and you coming home to her. It gives her a preview on how things could be. Also she'll start to expect for you to come over more often and to come over your place more often no matter the time of day.

Notes:

_____

_____

_____

_____

_____

_____

_____

_____

_____

_____

_____

_____

_____

_____

_____

LAW 43

Some Things Are Worth Repeating

Always reiterate to her what you want and don't want while dating. Women are emotional human beings. They function with their heart before their mind. A woman will say originally all she wants is to date, good conversation, physical attention, companionship, and nothing more serious than that.

Never believe that fellas because women aren't built like that. If a man gives a woman everything she asks, she has no choice but to catch feelings. This causes conflict between the man and woman because she will grow to expect more than what the initial agreement was.

Men, be honest about what you want while dating and run it back to her you're not looking for anything serious. Most men get pressured into relationships for it only to blow up in their faces later due to them not being ready.

Notes:

_____

_____

_____

_____

_____

_____

_____

_____

_____

_____

_____

_____

_____

_____

_____

_____

LAW 44

Stay In the
'Homie, Lover, Friend' Zone

When meeting women, a *mack* likes to keep the situation in a specific area. Just above the *"platonic friend zone"* and right under the *"relationship zone"* is where you can find the *"homie, lover, friend zone."*

The goal is to maintain and keep the situation within that middle area of the *"homie lover friend zone"* as long as you can without moving up or down. In this area you are just friends, but reap all the benefits of a relationship. The things that this area may consist of are companionship, an occasional date, quality time, and sex.

The quality time and occasional dating should be measured based off of what string she is on your roster. Some women could be content with staying in this area damn near forever, but most will eventually want that next level: the relationship zone.

If you tell her that's not something you want or looking for she may decide to stay hoping that she could eventually change your mind; otherwise it may always be an issue regarding a relationship. *If the issue persists, it may be time to call it quits.*

Notes:

_____

_____

_____

_____

_____

_____

_____

_____

_____

_____

_____

_____

LAW 45

Avoid Cuffing Season

There is a time of year that women like to reach out to any man for companionship. You don't even have to be in a relationship for them to want you during this time. They want all of your time and undivided attention. This dreaded time of year is called *cuffing season*.

Specifically I would say Cuffing Season is in the fall and winter months. It gets cooler not to mention the holidays: Thanksgiving, Christmas, New Years, and Valentine's Day many couples enjoy together. If you are talking to multiple women you will be getting pressured for companionship meaning quality time and gifts.

During these months be very family oriented even more so than usual. No woman can compete with family, especially your mother. Make it your business to give most of your time to your family during these months. Go visit family out of town. Be a part of family get-togethers as well as entertaining family or friends coming in from out of town.

No woman is that eager to meet your family and be bombarded with questions when the two of you aren't even exclusive. As far as Valentine's Day goes hopefully your mom or grandmother is still around you can pass them off as your Valentine; if not it'll be a great day to do some overtime at the job. If you're not trying to be cuffed avoid Cuffing Season by any means necessary.

Notes:

_____

_____

_____

_____

_____

_____

_____

_____

_____

LAW 46

Keep All of Your Things with You

By this time in your journey, it is obvious that you are sleeping over to her place from time to time, and she's sleeping at your place from time to time. We urge you to never leave any of your things at her house, and don't let her leave things at your house either.

You'll definitely catch hell getting your stuff back if things aren't sweet between you two. If you do leave stuff at her place, leave meaningless things. If there are no attachments between the both of you, it makes it easier to cut ties with each other when things don't work out. Trust us, you don't want there to be any reason for her to come pop up at your crib for anything or vice versa.

Women can be very spiteful and get real petty when you decide to leave them alone. Everything will be on her time when it involves you getting your belongings back. She'll even be as generous enough to take it upon herself to pop up to your crib to bring you your stuff just to be nosey or show out if you have company. Nine times out of ten your stuff is bleached, broken, or given away.

Women also like to mark their territory little by little leaving things at your crib for another woman to see it. When you're over her place be sure to take everything even when she says you could leave something. Going back over to her place after a fall out is just asking for trouble.

Notes:

_____

_____

_____

_____

_____

_____

_____

_____

_____

_____

LAW 47

Try Not To Burn Bridges

When you decide to cut ties with a woman, be sure to try not to burn bridges with her. She may be beneficial to you in the long run. When you decide to stop dating a woman, try to make it into a mutual decision.

Make her understand that you both get along better as friends and the timing is wrong for something more than that. Let her know if she ever needs anything don't hesitate to call. She'll definitely do the same and when that happens use her as a resource. For example, she may have connections or discounts for plane tickets, amusement parks, restaurants, hotels, etc.; all in which you could use to your advantage for another woman.

Don't hesitate to help her has well, only if it's within your power. Keep in contact with her for small talk and show her that you care about her wellbeing.

Be sure to keep her at a distance and not to double back for sex or a second stint in dating her. She is used strictly as a resource.

Notes:

_____

_____

_____

_____

_____

_____

_____

_____

_____

_____

_____

_____

LAW 48

If You Don't Mean It, Don't Say It

All of the information in this book is void if you have told the woman that you are dating that you love her. The laws in this book will not apply. Remember love is next level, which is beyond the dating aspect of things. When you are using the word LOVE you are now entering the relationship realm. More power to you if that's what you're ready for but be prepared to be a one woman man.

When you're just dating casually, never tell a woman that you love her because using that little word complicates and confuses the whole situation. Within the first few months, even though it's primarily infatuation that women feel, they often get it confused thinking that they are in love.

A lot of guys use the word love to easily get things they want from a woman. We know that this is unnecessary and could come back to bite you in your ass. If you tell a woman that you love her and don't mean it be prepared for the flood gates of hell to open up.

Women act on emotions, so hurting her after popping that word could mean pop ups to your house, or your job. It could bring on constant phone calls, or cause drama involving other women, or even lead her to vandalizing your car, and broadcasting your business on social media.

We suggest that you tell her that you aren't ready for love. Because often she'll respect it enough not to bring it up...or at least she'll wait a while before she does. If she feels that way she'll keep it to herself before telling you not risking the possibility of running you off.

Notes:

_____

_____

_____

_____

_____

_____

_____

_____

_____

LAW 49

Make sure You Are Not Mack'd

Believe it or not fellas, women are better Macks than us. There are more men thirsting over women than women thirsting over men. We often find ourselves doing so much to gain so little. When you start feeling like this while getting to know a woman, nine times out of ten you are getting *mack'd*.

If you're constantly going out of your way to accommodate her and everything is at her convenience, you're definitely getting *mack'd*. You must value yourself as much as she values herself. Make everything a compromise to where she has to give as well; whether it may be time, money, affection, respect, etc.

The thirst and attraction over a woman will have you careless enough to fall victim to the very laws you're supposed to abide by. Frequently refer back to the laws if you find yourself doing uncharacteristic things without even knowing this woman.

It's in a man's nature to go *"boo boo the fool"* over a woman when we first meet them. The laws act as a guideline to keep you grounded while you are casually dating. These laws help keep you from being taken advantage of: they keep you from getting *mack'd*.

Be careful because the same *Mack'n Almanac* laws that you follow can be used against you.

Notes:

_____

_____

_____

_____

_____

_____

_____

_____

_____

LAW 50

Mack'n Ain't Forever

The life of a *mack* isn't a forever lifestyle. This lifestyle is temporary, but can lead you to meeting a variety of interesting women. It leads you to figuring out what you want and don't want out of a woman. It could also lead you to love without that being any of your intentions. I don't care who you are, it's hard to deny a woman who has everything you ever wanted in a companion.

She may be a first string or a second string that moved up that you've been dealing with for a long time that you just can't shake the deep feelings for. If you have become a habitual offender of breaking the laws in this book when it comes to her and you don't even care; your *mack'n* days are over.

When being a habitual offender of breaking these laws have you looking at LIFE in marriage, your *mack'n* days are over permanently. There is nothing wrong with your *mack'n* days being over, but not accepting and acknowledging that your *mack'n* days are over is a problem. You could find a beautiful thing when *mack'n* or let a beautiful thing find someone else.

Fellas, it's OK if a particular woman starts to command most of your time and attention. Just make sure that it is the right woman who is causing you to break all of the *mack'n* laws. You need to recognize when this happens, and know when it is time to go to the next level, because by this time your actions and affection shown toward this woman, makes the laws of *The Mack'n Almanac* useless.

Notes:

_____

_____

_____

_____

_____

_____

_____

_____

_____

Bonus Information

Different Types of Women and How to Deal with Them

So far, you have a good background on our laws of the art of *mack'n*. We have brushed over some of details about the women that you will meet, but this bonus section gives you a head's up on some of the types of women that you will meet on your casual dating journey.

It is only fair that after we've armed you with the laws that you know some of the types of women that you will meet. When you know who they are, you will know how to finesse the situation and make informed decisions on how to deal with them or if you want to deal with them at all. Here we go:

Ms. Independent

This type of woman is educated, hardworking, self-sufficient and ambitious. Her goals are career oriented more than anything else. Of course she has all the materialistic things of the world because she feels that she deserves them. She loves to remind a man that she doesn't need him. One of her favorite quotes is: *"What can a man do for me that I can't do for myself?"*

So how would you approach this type of woman? First of all, don't feel intimidated by her success. It's hard for her to find a man that is as successful as her. Be confident when talking to her, but not conceited. Little things such as constant compliments, listening to her vent, constant affection, moral support, and being a gentleman at all times mean so much to this type of woman.

When we refer to constant affection, we mean foot rubs, massages, bubble baths, or even a home cooked candlelight dinner waiting for her when she gets home from work. Most of the guys that are just as successful as her won't do any of that. They think gifts and money can win her over, but that doesn't impress her because she can do that herself.

The last sure way in winning her over would be the sex. Most likely this woman has never had out of the ordinary type sex. Same old positions and in the same old places describes her all the way, but she does have a freak in her, which she is dying to bring out. Have sex with her in all ways that are possible and in spontaneous places. If you fulfill her up most fantasies then she'll be sprung.

After that she could give a damn about how much you make. If anything she'll want to make you happy and would go the extra mile to help you achieve your goals.

Ms. Insecure

Every woman has her own insecurities. Some women are more insecure than others. Your job is to find out her insecurities and free her from them. Her insecurities could come from her past experiences with men. It could be her physical appearance, her financial situation, kids, or her own promiscuous past.

Make her feel comfortable and show her that you accept her the way she is. Her confidence will build once you show her that whatever she is insecure about doesn't matter to you. Shine the spotlight on her good qualities, accomplishments, and make her feel beautiful inside and out no matter what. Whatever that may be broken or broken down inside of her, you make it your business to fix it and build it back up.

Most guys just let women deal with their insecurity issue themselves and don't show that they genuinely care. Take an interest in why she does the things she do and work on improving it little by little. This will raise her self-esteem and she'll put you above any man she has ever dealt with. You will impact her forever.

Ms. Damaged Goods

It takes a big man to take on this type of woman. It takes a whole lot of patience, time, determination, and persistence to change her perception of a man. She is angry and spiteful from her past experiences with men. Years of cheating, lies, and deceit made her outside hard as a rock; But once you crack the outer layer her inner layer is soft as cotton.

She can be everything you ever wanted or needed in a woman and more. Trust me the benefits can be endless if you're strong enough to endure the outer layer.

The outer layer consists of constant comparisons to exes, constant regrets/reflections on past issues, trust issues, unnecessary petty arguments and attitudes. All of those are defense mechanisms to detour you from getting to the inner layer, which is her heart. A lot of times this pushes good quality men away and then she resorts back to the men of her past that made her into *Ms. Damaged Goods* in the first place.

Remember damaged doesn't make her irreparable, fellas. She's only damaged beyond repair if she resorts back to the men of her past or the same type of men that made her that way. If she's worth it turn into *Mr. Fix It*.

Ms. Cougar

This woman is older, experienced, and preys particularly on the younger male. She has done the long, drawn out, serious relationships, and isn't looking for one. She probably even has been married and divorced. She's looking for a younger guy to make her feel youthful, bring her excitement, and give her new experiences.

A man should stay in control when dealing with this type of woman, but not overbearing to where she feels you're trying to run her. Just in control of the situation. Give her time but don't spoil her with it because she'll expect a yes every time she calls. Make her feel like a young school girl again every time you link up by making her laugh, show her public displays of affection, always compliment her, etc.

With this woman she'll probably be fronting the bill on everything you do just to spend time with you. She'll show you things you have never experienced and you'll show her new things she has never experienced. Great sex on top of the way you're making her feel will have her head gone. Be careful because her feelings may come into play and relationship talk might come up.

Bring up your goals in life such as kids and marriage so that those conversations will simmer down, bringing her back to reality. *Ms. Cougar* has done the marriage thing and has already had her kids so that's out of the question. Dealing with this woman can be short term or long term. Eventually you'll get bored or tired of it, and the arrangement you two will have is over. It was fun while it lasted though.

Ms. Clingy

She's a very needy woman who needs your undivided attention at all times which consists of talking/texting all day, needs to have physical attention from you in public all the time, and never gets tired or enough of you. Most of these women are vulnerable and are fresh out of a relationship looking for someone to feel that void. Also it could be a woman that is used to being in a relationship so much that she doesn't know how to date.

These women get so infatuated with the first man with potential that comes along, that their natural instinct is to lock in quickly smothering a man. The average man probably would run, but the *mack's* approach would be to slow her down to your pace. Always dictate the pace of things. Make her aware of your schedule and of important things you have going on within your life. As a matter of fact, put her on a schedule.

When you do this, she will enjoy and cherish the time you do spend with her so much that she is willing to accept whatever time you can offer her. Make her feel that you're more than worth the wait and that it benefits both of you more not to rush spending time together. Tell her you don't want things to get old between you two and that every time you get together you want it to feel like the first time.

Ms. Controlling

This type of woman may come across as domineering, aggressive, stubborn, arrogant, and self-centered. She preys on weak men who might be so infatuated with her look that they don't realize what's really going on. She expects everything to happen on her time. Her interests are supposed to take priority over yours. The words *compromise* and *understanding* are completely foreign to her; they are not a part of her vocabulary.

Don't let this discourage you because you can flip the script on this type of woman easily. However, this is not a woman for the faint of heart; you have to be mentally strong to deal with this woman. Be prepared for a lot of debating or back and forth discussions. Show her the meaning of *compromise* by making her give something to get something. This shows her she can't always have it all and that you have to give a little to get a little. That could relate to time, money, and casual dating.

Everything shouldn't always happen on her time, spending your money, and always going where she wants. Make her give up at least one of the three. Also show her the meaning of *understanding* by constantly telling her to put herself in your shoes. Make her relate to how she makes you feel regarding the way she treats you. She'll probably get quiet, and then acknowledge that she was wrong. That's the hardest thing for this type of woman to do because they're so used to being right, that it makes them feel defeated to admit they're wrong.

Ms. Drama

This type of woman has a life filled with drama. It could stem from her child's father, her falling out with friends or family, crazy ex-boyfriends/girlfriends, money, and even legal issues. It seems like she embraces the drama because she keeps putting herself in all of these avoidable situations. Her life is always complicated due to not just her past mistakes, but making the same mistakes over and over again. We see her as having to learn everything the hard way, but the fact of the matter is she never learns.

We can't explain this, but there are some guys who actually will tolerate this type of woman. Our advice from personal experience is to *run*. All of the problems and issues that we've listed above will instantly become yours when you choose to deal with *Ms. Drama*.

She uses the sympathy role to prey on men who have a hard time saying no. Everybody goes through trials and tribulations in life, but the objective is to learn from them. *Ms. Drama* never learns. Instead of her fixing what is broken in her life, she'll use you as a crutch to help her get by even if it's only temporarily.

Here are examples of the kind of situations this type of woman will put you in if you are not careful:

Example 1: The guy *Ms. Drama's* on and off with in a dysfunctional relationship totaled her car in an accident. If you get caught up with her, she'll use you as the guy who's giving her rides to work when she's "off" from the main guy.

Example 2: You could be at her house relaxing and end up having your life threatened or car vandalized by her *ex* because she still wants to be "friends" with them.

Example 3: She is receiving little to any money from her child's father, but is constantly asking you for money for kids that aren't even yours.

Example 4: She may not even have seen her child's father in forever, but wants to fight his other kid's mother over something petty.

As we said earlier, we suggest that you run from this type of woman, but the only benefit from dealing with a woman like this is probably for great sex. To be honest, even if she can't do anything else for you, she may give you the best sex you have ever had. If that is the case and you decide to go this route based off of that reason alone, we highly suggest that you proceed with extreme caution. A lot of men get *trapped* in situations with Ms. Drama because they were suckered in based off of great sex, but they fail to realize they could be getting themselves wrapped up in a never ending world of drama.

Ms. Unhappily Married

This type of woman is seeking something she isn't receiving at home from her husband and usually it's attention. When things are going south in a marriage it seems like the husband isn't paying enough attention to the wife to even realize that he is losing her.

She's in limbo not knowing if she wants to continue the marriage, and he's distracted by other things brushing off her frustrations or her cries for help. *Ms. Unhappily Married* wants to vent to someone, spend time with someone, experience some excitement, get some affection, and have great sex unlike she has ever experienced or hasn't had in a very long time.

Ms. Unhappily Married welcomes any man willing to pay her any kind of attention the right way. Of course you would have to approach her like any other woman, which means respectfully and being courteous. Compliments go along way with her because she doesn't get that at home.

Ms. Unhappily Married is most comfortable with guys she has had a history with such as a coworker, classmate, friend of a friend, or even friend of the family. I'm not saying random guys don't have a chance; it's just a little harder because she needs to feel comfortable being with you. If you are the random guy and have approached a married woman that is still entertaining you even after she has disclosed her marital status, you have gotten her attention. There is something about you that she likes and that her husband doesn't have, used to have, or never did have at all.

The key is to keep her in her limbo stage, and make sure she does not have a hidden agenda to make your relationship more than what it is. You want this woman to stay at the stage in which she doesn't know what she wants to do within her marriage. She doesn't know if she wants to stay or leave because her mind and heart are going in two totally different directions. All she knows is that she enjoys your time and loves how you make her feel. You give her your undivided attention in every way possible. You listen to her vent about her frustrations and you relieve her stress by all means necessary. Try to stay off the subject of her marriage unless she brings it up. One thing about this situation is she can't expect it to be more than what it is, but that won't stop her from entertaining the thought.

Ms. Social Media

This type of woman absolutely can't go a second without posting her personal business online. It could be where she's going, what she's doing, what she's wearing, what she's eating, how she's feeling, selfie here and selfie there, who's she's with, "I'm bored," etc. Maybe she's seeking the approval or acceptance of others by constantly putting her business on *Front Street*. Be aware that she even puts her dating life, whether it's good or bad, out there for everyone to see.

If you are getting to know *Ms. Social Media*, make it known to her that you are a low key and private type of guy. Let her know that you're not big on social networking and you don't like to let a lot of people in your business. Trust us, if you don't let her know this in the beginning, you'll be included in her obsession, and this could throw a wrench in any plans for your casual dating life.

Everywhere you go, she has to take a picture to post on social media. This alerts everyone in her circle and yours of where you are and who you are with. Your life with her will be made public and you aren't even in a relationship with her. While you're getting to know her, everyone on social media is getting to know you post by post.

If things go sour, she'll definitely do the same as well. Some guys like the attention, but if she isn't your girlfriend this is all bad publicity. It makes you undesirable to quality women because they think you are taken. Some other women don't care if you are taken or not, but those aren't the caliber of women you want.

The message is you don't want other women to get to know you or your interests by someone else's posts; you want them to get to know you personally for themselves. You can know damn near everything about *Ms. Social Media* just from her daily posts and when you meet her you can simply act like you guys have so much in common. You already know her likes and dislikes. It's like she has given you the answers to her test.

Ms. Nightlife

Most likely you've met *Ms. Nightlife* in her natural setting, which is the club. You will definitely catch her there every weekend, every other weekend, and possibly some nights out of the week. That's what she looks forward to outside of her everyday responsibilities if she even has any responsibilities. It's almost as if she can't function outside that environment. She is the woman's number that you got that night and when you try to talk to her throughout the week all she wants to do is talk about that night at the club; and the next night she's going out.

There's really no substance to the conversations. On her social media pages notice the majority of her pictures revolve around the nightlife. Her pictures consist of her pre-club preparation, on her way to the club, her actually being in the club, and her after the club.

Now a lot of guys make the mistake of trying to take *Ms. Nightlife* seriously, but she can't be tamed. She can only be when she is ready; so with that being said treat her as she deserves. Only contact her on your time and "nightlife" hours. She is the perfect late night creep because she is always up coming from a club or party late night hours.

Also *Ms. Nightlife* isn't limited to partying within her city. You will catch her wherever the next party, festival, or shows are. If you happen to be there, I would hit her up as a last resort if you haven't met anyone new.

Notes:

_____

_____

_____

_____

_____

_____

_____

_____

Epilogue

As you embark on your journey in the casual dating world, we have armed you with the laws to succeed with different types of women, in different environments, in many different ways.

When you study these laws and execute them successfully you have transformed from Man to Mack; but of course just as in everything in life has a balance, this has to have balance as well.

Just like a sports team has an offense there has to be a defense. Fellas you didn't really expect us to leave the ladies out here defenseless did you?

All of these laws giving you the advantage over these defenseless women wouldn't be fun or fair; therefore, watch out for *HER MACK'N ALMANAC: 50 Laws of Casual Dating Just for Her* coming soon.

About the Authors

Slick Lemons was born and raised in Tampa, Florida. Raised as an only child by a single mother, Slick was immersed in the culture that allowed him to see women making things happen every day. Greatly influenced by his upbringing, Slick developed an intuitive gift for understanding the heart, and mind of women.

Slick also credits the advice and guidance he received from real life *macks* for helping him sharpen his ability to provide insightful contributions to *The Mack'n Almanac*. Slick skillfully gleans from these influential relationships, and experiences from years of casually dating a variety of women to co-author The Mack'n Almanac and launch additional entertainment ventures.

* * *

Montez (Tezz) Watson was also born and raised in Tampa, Florida. Tezz was raised by a single mother and grew up in public housing where he was exposed to and witnessed a lot at an early age. Tezz took heed to the stories older neighborhood *macks* often told about their exploits with multiple women. Inquisitive and engaging as a youth, Tezz found it easy to interact with people of any age and backgrounds. This skill made it easier for him to converse with young women who found him to be a comfortable retreat from the typical awkward hustle from other teen boys.

As a teen, Tezz used the words and information he gained from listening to older *macks* to sharpen his ability to communicate with members of the opposite sex at local teen night parties, school and neighborhood events. As he matured, Tezz found himself regularly giving advice on women to his male friends and family members. He began to journal about the scenarios and the advice he gave, which led to the development and co-authoring of *The Mack'n Almanac*.

Published by:

M.A.I.N. ENTERTAINMENT, LLC.
www.MainENT.co

www.ingramcontent.com/pod-product-compliance
Lightning Source LLC
Chambersburg PA
CBHW071132280326
41935CB00010B/1193